MYSTERIOUS LIGHT
POEMS, COLORFUL AND TRANSPARENT

BY
JOYCE SANDRA UHLIR

BLUE LIGHT PRESS ◆ 1ST WORLD PUBLISHING

1ˢᵗ WORLD
PUBLISHING

SAN FRANCISCO ◆ FAIRFIELD ◆ DELHI

Mysterious Light
Poems, Colorful and Transparent

1st World Publishing
809 South 2nd Street
Fairfield, Iowa 52556
www.1stworldpublishing.com

Blue Light Press
1563 45th Avenue
San Francisco, California 94122

Cover and Book Design
Melanie Gendron
www.melaniegendron.com

Cover Painting
Bones of Zion
© by Joyce Sandra Uhlir

Photo of Painting
Kelly Kowall
ckgsm@yahoo.com

First Edition

LCCN: 2010931599

ISBN: 9781421891583

Acknowledgments:

I would like to thank the many people who have supported and encouraged my desire to write. To Diane Frank I owe the most, for her skill in understanding learning styles and the ability to guide me through a form of expression using word paint.

A big thanks to Sylvia Beaupre from New Hampshire and Bonnie Jenko from Waukesha Wi. who proofread and checked punctuation. A really big thanks to Teddi Bianchi, a long time friend who spent years going over poems for typos and punctuation. She not only proofread but was a constant encouragement.

To all my on line friends from Blue light Press, too numerous over the years to mention, a big thank you. A few, like Judy Liese and Devorah Rubin, have been special friends for more than four years now.

Special thoughts for their encouragement are Dawn Hoffman, Helen Moser, Jim and Sally Mergener, Debbie and Lenny Kimmel, Kery Kafka, Irene and Hank Woods, Jackie and Frank Sylvia, Helene Heffner, Julie Teliz, Linda Herscher, my brother George and of course my son, Todd.

A special mention for Norma Dudley and Jake Williams who have moved on to a world reserved for all of us. They were my greatest fans and avid readers. To both of them I have dedicated the Poem, "When all the Veils are Lifted."

A special thanks as well to my Tuesday morning group from Caribbean Isles writers group. Elad Laems, Don Miner, Marian Howcroft, Al Wheeler, David Oliver and John Foster, who attended faithfully each week with new poems to share and constructive comments. A special thanks to the Sun City's poet group meeting each month. Special mention of Annie Hunter who founded the group.

This book is dedicated with love and much affection
to my son Todd Uhlir
who resides in The Woodlands, Texas.
His love for fishing and sports is inherited.
We have a close bond with a shared faith
that centers our relationship.

Table of Contents

"Painting is poetry that is seen
rather than felt,
and poetry is painting
that is felt rather than seen."

—Leonardo da Vinci

Bones of Zion

I ink the skeleton of a silver leaf poplar
with a roller and black ink.
Careful to overlap, I print rock designs
into a cerulean sky.

Mixing a mango blush,
I paint between spaces
formed on stretched fabric.
Bright sunlight, rain and wind
bare the surface to the feel of silk.

Deep textures of pink from grapefruit
wash into shadows.
The deep reds of cranberry
find their way into crevices
causing rocks to leap onto the canvas.

Below, rivers vein their way
through dark umber flesh
dressed in oxides and olive green foliage.

The doors of evening close.
Distant stones in a dark universe
blink a light
burning white in my chest.

Frozen Forest

Norway pines,
sheltered in whipped cream blankets,
dot the hills of northern Wisconsin.
Green needles sleep
under white covers,
edges crocheted in loose knit patterns.

As spring arrives
with a wet snowfall,
songs crackle from weary branches.
Heavy comforters avalanche the forest floor,
limbs relieved of burdens.

Two field mice race to a nearby log;
a red fox sits washing his face,
too full from an early breakfast
to take up the chase.
Footprints profile earlier wanderings.

I cross a path worn by deer hooves
in search of tender roots beneath the snow.
Rabbit tracks lead to a hole
where a mother scurried
to escape being lunch.

My square-toed boots sink deep
into the soft whiteness;
prints shadow close behind.

In the distance, I hear trees
releasing winter's memories.
I float to the edge of their voices,
but hear only sounds of footsteps.

WILL OF THE WIND

Our boat dances with blustery air currents
swinging in curtsied bows.
Rods and reels balance on the edge of oars.
Lines dangle over the edge
baited with wiggling night crawlers.
We pleasure in the wait.

My son and I share silent moments
as I tiptoe the edge of thought.
Observing the sun bathing his nose,
moisture beading its surface—
his wet face beautiful, framed in daydreams.

As the wind changes directions,
I am moved to past memories
of a small boy planting wet kisses on my lips.
Flavors of peanuts and raspberry linger,
little fingers touching my eyelashes
investigating the holes in my ears;
cheeks soft as flowering bluebell tongues.

Stirred by the timbre in his voice,
remembering Puff the Magic Dragon
sung in the key of C;
painful cries when the sidewalk found his knee,
laughter when a bluegill captured his bait
dancing in the air—until, with a thud,
it lands in my lap among fits of joy.

Textured Words

I sit on a flat rock
to watch blue and gold of day
slowly disappear into night.

A loon, silhouetted
against the last orange sliver of evening,
searches for her mate.
My breathing stops
as I fall off the edge of her cries.

The sky rips open
to let her song pass by,
touching rocks, trees and me.

In shadows, I am textured
with sounds of joy and sorrow,
left to wonder how such beauty found a home.

Could an oboe sing those expressive notes?
Can I paint them in warm colors?

I focus on her sculptured elegance
in black and white.
Feelings texture simple words
wrapping me inside a song.

Sacred Valley

Sun washes across California hills
uncovering blankets of green.
Yellow heads from dandelions
sway back and forth.

Deep reds from merlot grapes
mixed with avocado-colored vines
hang from arbors.
Sweet smells drift into stag horn sumac.

Words spill from my lips.
Each sound grabbed by a breeze
carried through a cloud of blackbirds
to bounce off the side of a ravine.

Swallowed by the mouth of a cave,
it boomerangs back
to wrap around me,
not once, but two or three times.
Earth and sky sing a musical round.

I balance on the rim of each word
until the canyon's breath is spent.
Echoes cling with silent fingers.

Streaked with Silver

I kick the wheel beneath my feet,
a potter's table spins between my knees.
Hands wet with slip
bring a mound of gray clay to symmetrical.

Fingers shape and reshape,
pinch and pull
until...
a bowl discovers its size and shape.
A flared rim balances the top.
It dries on a wooden rack.

Covered in pink and gray glazes,
placed in a kiln to endure the fire of change,
reds and oranges emerge,
its persona established forever.

Sitting on the soft edges of night,
the moon god fills me
with a silver glow;
flesh textured with joie de vivre,
hair streaked with silver.

I watch the moon nip at the heels of dusk
in a race that can't be won.

Filial Thread

Under early morning pink clouds
black winged ravens circle,
mirrored off the surface of a pond.
Brown cattails stand alert
around edges blended with saw-tooth grass.

Flat, green lily pads float
on the surface
attached by a long cord
to the womb;
sanctuary for water walkers, spiders and dragonflies,
a tasty lunch for waiting bass.

When the lavender curtain of sunset is drawn,
night is presented with a chorus
of unsynchronized voices.
Each sing a song of rebirth.

Wind howls like a woman in labor
as mother earth struggles
against abortion from acid rain.

Will the circling sentinels
call out warnings of doom
before they see themselves echoed
off shattered pieces of glass?

Passing Through Flames

A varnished desk top,
initials carved into its glossy surface,
resting place for paper, pencils and elbows.
Feet barely able to touch the floor,
my daily prison.

A nearby window offers escape
for hurtful rejections to float out.
Eyes focused on nothing,
I am able to see everything
in my hidden world of daydreams;
fantasized tales of a nine-year-old
played on a movie screen.

A shadow crosses before unseeing eyes,
my name called to spell words aloud:
"....to....be....so....it".
A stranger called "superintendent,"
judge of all two-letter words,
waits in silence—the class looked on.

Not able to spell,
I was directed to an office
where tests grew like puddles in a rainstorm.
Judgment sat in a gray suit
while anxious parents spun justifications
into armor to protect the family name.

"Slow learner, delayed, unable to read,
not like her twin brother, not college material."
Names burned into my flesh
like initials carved into my desk.

A grin fills corners of my mouth
turning pencils to brushes,
paper to canvas.
Mangos and oranges dance on my palette.

Mirrored Worlds

At the matrix of early morning,
an orchestra plays among hues
of indigo and orange.
Tenor and bass notes amuse themselves
inside a breeze.
Leaves shiver into the soft roll of a snare.

Beneath wispy strands of awareness,
clouds race across cornfields
into the teals of distant mountains.
Corn stalks wave in passing.
Golden silk falls across my pillow.

Jasmine plays at the tip of my nose.
Cranberries splash around
the playfulness of my tongue
as sea gulls call through darkened corridors
of my dreams.

I pick fairy dust
off the black fabric of night
and place them in a world
that now lives in me.

Seamless Moments

Growing up, I observed time
spin my mother's clock
from thirty-nine to ninety-two.

Her skin, elastic at forty
like a nylon stretched over her calf.
Opaque in texture;
a burnt umber from the sun
moisturized by cream from a Ponds' jar
on her vanity.

I watched my father stroke
her arms with his eyes.
We never touched one another.

During her declining years,
nurses bathed her
in lavender light from evening,
careful not to break tissue paper skin,
blue veined spider webs laid out
like underground rivers
beneath a translucent surface.

Pools of blood seen in black and blue
leak under a thin membrane;
bumps from supper trays or bed stand edges.

I squint into the mirror.
Glasses slip down my nose
magnifying tiny waves
moving out of corners of eyes and mouth,
spreading across my face.

MIRACLE OF A TOUCH

I watch an eagle's head crowned in white
blink silver and russet
in reflections from a setting sun.
Her golden corneas hold vertical layers
of volcanic glass,
mirrors that see into darkness
known only to the moon.

Her fledglings wait at the top of a nearby birch.

Looking down, she searches
for an evening meal,
a rabbit or squirrel,
hiding among undulating,
ghost-like shadows
from swaying branches.

Her yellow, hooked beak opens
in a piercing cry, slicing an opening
for her ascent into a painting by Purcell.
Talons dipped in a palette
of magenta, creams and gold
paint the bottom edges of indigo cumulus.

My mother's unsettled spirit
wanders, unattached, from neglect as a child,
searching—always searching
for the warm touches of evening colors.

The eagle returns to her nest,
soaring on gray wings tipped in silver
to feed and nurture her young.

LOVE STORY IN PAINT

Windflowers in flaring skirts
waltz in my painted garden.
Red and blue anemones overlap,
splashing in pools
of blended violets and lavenders.
Leaves whisper
about bees and honey.

I call for locust wings
to fly me to the top of green aspen
to watch colors give birth;
stars arriving
with the first yawn of evening.
I sing a lullaby with ripples
from a nearby brook,
touch stamens of bluebells
and watch yellow pollen explode
into the life cycle
of another spring.

Music Among the Flowers

Mom said to live above a funeral home
meant quiet times,
only whispers allowed.
No feet must touch the floor
when a showing is in progress.
I have grown to believe that meant
"viewings of the dead," usually seven to ten,
bedtime for children.
I lay and listened, no one to talk with.

Hail Mary, Full of Grace.
Voices, rising like helium
traveling through floorboards
rest on my ears.
Services for someone begin;
prayers and hope given
to remove the sting from loss.

Crying and repentant moans
mixed with smells from carnations
drifted upward
trapped with me in my silent tomb.
Landscapes from lives changing forever.

I attend to another sound, soft
like cotton, a bubbling brook.
Notes from our Hammond organ embrace me.
My plaything, my passion,
my way to escape from tragedy.

Our silent guests, passing through,
hands folded pending a final bouquet
of roses and baby's breath,
listened to one last concert.

FULL CIRCLE

I remember how fires burned
in the pre-dawn of arousal
climbing to the summit's peak
where affirmations of ecstasy
dislodge from my throat.

Lying on my back, knees bent,
feet strapped into stirrups,
I pushed down.
Stomach muscles contracted
like wet leather left to the sun.
My swollen womb igniting screams
of primal avowals;
howling winds in a storm.

My arms, a cradle made of flesh,
waited to embrace new life.
Wails penetrated stillness
as need called to need giver.
Breasts, heavy with milk,
replaced cries with sounds of suckling.

Nearby, a lace curtain drawn
through twilight's shadows
waits for one last breath.
The final thread unraveling life
into an audible sigh,
carried back to where it began.

A Love Affair with Music

I am told our universe is soundless;
no noises from exploding stars
or planets whirling
like my childhood red top with yellow stripes,
whistling when it spins in circles.
I cannot hear meteors crash together
or comets swishing though black holes.

Yet—this morning I wake to a symphony.
Distant kettledrums thunder,
then slowly wane.
Cymbals crash at just the right moment.

Snare drums reach a full crescendo
as raindrops rap and tap
on my window, in my backyard
and on the roof.

Violins and the bass viol play touch tag,
humming through branches,
dodging around giant oaks to play deep tones.
Leaves stir into a frenzy of high-pitched chords,
squeezing through a crack
in my bedroom window in F sharp.

A cello and longbow ribbon themselves near my pillow.
My yearning for the magic of music implodes.
A star spent, falls into silence.

Transparent Moments

Your laughter wove magic around me.
Little dancing fingertips tickled my flesh
as we played back and forth with humor.
Smells of Old Spice still linger.

I would move into your guarded space,
face schooled in the art of pretense
to observe your tongue sneaking
past corners of your mouth
for fragments of words left unsaid.

Eyes, a light blue pond
of quivering movement,
held thoughts in their depths,
too far away to be recovered.
I played instead with twinkles
that burned white in their corners.

A tear often rolled down your cheek
covering stains left from a moment of joy
when you watched your son
breathe his first breath,
unaware you would not be there
to watch him grow.

Your stature filled my sky from east to west,
captured inside a prism of crimson light
in a fading afternoon.

Stories in Season

Last fall, soft maple leaves feathered
   to the ground;
   blankets piled high
   in rusts and reds.

This spring after winter's reprieve,
   bridal wreath frolic
   in white, floral wedding gowns,
   renewing marriage vows.

Memories of rebirth
   reflect in the golds of dawn;
   stories retold beneath shades
   of an ultramarine evening.

Nearby a soft voice
   textured with the quiver of age
   spins tales of green dragons.
   Children parachute
   from dandelions, aged in white,
   onto playgrounds of make-believe.

SURFACING

With wet hands
I mold, contour and give feelings to clay
mounted on a sculpture table.
You pose nearby,
a book of unread pages.

My hands span trapezius muscles,
move over firmness of deltoids,
feel male strength beneath my finger tips.
I shape and reshape lids and lashes
over colorless eyes,
prisoners to unknown emotions.

Struggling for perfection,
I rework your nose with my thumbs.
A red fingernail defines edges.
Hands dipped in a bowl of slip
transfer silk to soften skin.

I cup your face with both hands,
thumbs working contours of lips
adding textures of thought.
Little fingers find the crease
where they almost part.
Gentle in my caresses,
I measure their fullness.
They speak to me from the belly of a sigh.

Your thoughts etched in shadows
now fully clothed,
or are those my feelings of pleasure
fashioned across your face.

Tongue of Fire

My lips, once moist,
cool to the touch,
now throb,

ablaze from the sun's
sultry rays,
scorched to strawberry red.

Swollen and cracked,
my tongue seeks their relief...
then lingers,

wetting the surfaces
to cool the pain.

A deception slipped
from between my lips
to burn again
this tender mouth.

My tongue, turned viper,
is now unable to cool flames
of the foolish
and is left to wrestle
with the dread
of discovery.

INNOCENCE IN MY POCKET

On my bug-proof screen porch
I enjoy a novel by Grisham.
Short Tail, a tan chipmunk
with black designer stripes down his back,
takes up summer residence with me.
He has a secret entrance.

Unsalted peanuts fill my shirt pocket,
so he loves me very much.
Scampering up my bare legs
leaving tattoos in white from sharp toes;
little brown droppings brushed away
with a flip of my hand.

He dives into my pocket
surfacing with bulging cheeks,
scampering away to a hole
only he knows where
to store his winter's cache.

When his hunger needs are met
he sits on my book, washes his face
while I scratch above his cut-off tail;
his face changing to white, like my hair.

When the birth of spring celebrates shades of green,
I call out his name.
Only robins and blue jays respond,
each in their own language.
Pages turn from whispering winds
who share with me his resting place
among his final hoard of peanuts.

20

Lost in Time

My lips part to frame
the silence of redwoods.
Eyes feast on root-textured trunks
mounting upward
into motionless branches.

Green canopies structure the tops.
Sunlight bleaches through.
Gold and yellow threads of light spool
to the forest floor
slipping past giant trunks
painted in blends of burnt umber and red.
An aurora borealis shimmers inside the past.

I wait for this ancient world to find me
while I journey on wings of monarchs,
hovering over lady ferns of cadmium,
resting on yellow flowers
whose name is lost to my age.

A faint breeze brushes across my cheek
to cool the wonder
around a timeless world of giants.

Bitter Mixed with Sweet

Head propped against a feather pillow
I listen to the Boston Pops
play "Dance of the Flowers."
Flutes and clarinets chase one another
up and down musical refrains.
Moisture from joy seeps through my lashes.

The mood changes character
when bows drawn across strings
of violins, cellos and basses
release mournful cries,
a reminder of love torn away
in a death visited too soon.
A wet drop rolls from hiding.

I sniff orange blossoms covered in pollen.
My eyes resent the intrusion
with sniffles escaping behind a sneeze.
Stinging sea serpents swim around my eyelids
from cutting onions for chicken soup.

I slipped off the edges of composure
when my son kissed my cheek,
leaving home when his man image called,
phoning years later to say, "Mom I love you."
My tears released in silence.

MOON CATCHERS

Mother closes the door
leaving my bedroom painted in black.
Knocks, scratches and moans
sneak through cracks in the window.
I wonder if spirits live nearby.

I feel my way around the bed,
along the metal bedstead,
fingers searching for the crocheted ring
that hangs from my window shade.
I give a quick tug,
release, and listen
as it spins in frantic circles to the top.

I watch the moon search
for holes to blink through,
swimming straight to the big elm tree,
slipping past clumps of dried leaves
through my bedroom window
and onto the wall in transparent
shades of gray
crafting strange masks with large eyes,
vacant mouths and cobwebbed hair.
Ghost-like they swing their arms
and dance in circles.

Shadows fade
when night turns its face towards the sun
and sleep throws off the covers.

A New Beginning

The sun moves in slow motion
towards dawn.
A kitten stalks white mist
and playful shadows of early morning.
Hillsides bathe in lavenders and yellows.

Amethyst crystals explode
as they dance off ripples in a pond.
A golden lion ascends on cushioned paws
into my dreamscape.

Curtains drawn over my eyes,
skin soaking up warm morning radiance,
kisses whisper across my skin.
In my throat, a cat's purr escapes.

I browse near the surface of dreams
not hearing intrusive knocks
or voices calling through a veil of desires.
I am drawn into the stillness
of early morning.

Subtle Changes

I walk into a dense forest,
listen to sparrows and crows welcome me
with soft chirps and loud squawks.
Oak leaves kited in greens
whisper until night shadows unfold
in weeping edges of ash.
Katydids, locusts and crickets hum,
a cryptogram to the rebirth of life.

A sprawling elm with textured bark
once scratched my hands.
Now soft, fuzzy moss captures my touch,
oxide green by day, a ghoulish ash by night.
It creeps like my age, without notice.

The moon nestles in a cradle of darkness.
A silver glow reflects off names and dates
etched into smooth surfaces
of pink and hoary stones.
I am left to wonder
how many nights have come and gone
in my five times fifteen years.

I reminisce about these woods
wondering if I will remember shapes and sizes
of pines, oaks and poplars,
for time moves quickly
with slippers on her feet.

WALKING THE EDGE

A white shawl hugs me
in evening's blue-violet sky.
I search for galaxies that neighbor my thoughts
of journeys taken and those to come.

It is difficult to remember
how many times an orange sun slipped
over my morning window sill
or the silver glow of moonlight
pressed thin,
squeezed under the front door.
I have not counted poems written
nor do I remember their names,
yet each one holds my fingerprint.

I trace hems on my many gowns
with knowing fingers,
reflect on faces sculptured with my eyes.
Hair aged white, a dried dandelion
waits for an evening breeze

LEGACY

Snuggling beneath a tan sheet and blanket,
a warm and soft cocoon,
I search for a latch
to open my window back to awareness.

Dreaming, I kiss damp lips of tulips
from early morning dewdrops.
I imagine the hawked throats of snapdragons
with white faces and pink tongues
towering on a stem
singing alto and soprano duets.

In front of me, a lush forest
in vibrant mantles of jade and lime
sway like violin bows
in a visual symphony.

Hearing voices,
I am drawn back to consciousness,
alarms sounding for a planet fractured.
Carbon footprints tiptoe in the shadows.

A Taste of Beautiful

A monarch butterfly lights on my arm
as I breathe in flowered fields.
I welcome her gentle touch
as she sips moisture from my skin.

A caterpillar transforms
into a tissue paper mosaic;
wings made of burnt orange shapes
framed in black, quiver in the wind.

I watch her seek the beauty
of buddleia flowers
and yellow petals of Black-eyed Susans,
tasting sweetness from colorful differences.

She shares with me the nectar
of her femininity,
laying eggs under the leaves
of milkweed pods;
a beginning life cycle
in a journey back to beautiful.

Fear Dissolves into Silence

Cumulus clouds with chubby white faces
and pink crocheted edges
drift across blue skies.
I watch twilight flee towards night
and feel unafraid.

Turning towards the east,
clouds painted in grays, tower upward.
Panic surfs across my flesh
watching white light split the sky.
Aggression races,
bending low the tops of trees.
Echoed sounds of kettle drums and cymbals
frame them into nightmares.

I am poured to the top with fear.
Powerful winds build into violence
gathering screams to throw at the moon.

Furnaces with tall chimneys
impale the horizon
spewing dark ash over humankind.
Fear takes refuge under blankets;
courage to speak tucked
into deep folds of pillows.

Wind Songs

Smiles gust through me
as fall leaves arrive
in yellows, rusts and reds.
Strong breezes lift them into the air,
swirl them around my feet
until they settle to the ground
in colorful mosaics.

In a merciless frenzy,
branches whip,
knock on my kitchen window.
Boat sails billow,
even oat fields bend their heads.
Wide brimmed hats find new neighbors.

My front door blows wide open,
tumbling the welcome mat into the hall,
turning newspapers into kites.
An invisible presence whispers past,
leaving me to wonder.

Lobster Poem—Say What?

I graze pages of Webster's dictionary
searching for the Lobster;
"a hard-shelled sea crustacean with a pair of pincers,
two pair of antennae, eyes on the end of stalks,
with a hard shell covering."
The perfect subject for a poem.
I am left to develop this lonely alien into verse
that carries with it no fuzzy touches or pulsing pain.
Or does it?

My imagination runs with the wind
leaping over rocks and fallen birch logs
to grasp an idea.
Toying with it like a baby kitten,
rolling words around a salivating tongue,
tasting the sweet white meat of joy
against the roof of my mouth.

Overwhelmed, I lean against a daydream
on a crystal white sea shore.
Phrases like "soft and delicate,
dipped into melted butter, and lips set aflame"
play a game of hide and seek
among conchs, starfish and abalone shells
bleached white from the sun.

I wake up from this brief trance
to discover my poem, body and subtext have vanished.
A trail of visceral phrases,
alchemical-dipped words with images dragged
on their way back to the ocean.

DANCING SILVER BIRCH

Around the edges of our lake
birch trees huddle
where richness of soil blends with sand.
White bark circles slender trunks.
Black lines and dark spots draw my eyes
into an ink wash.

Early spring buds metamorphose
into leaves of olive and cadmium
while night's faint sliver of moon glow
spray paints the undersides gray.
When dark retreats from light,
leaves, like highlighted hair, wink silver.

When the morning God Zephyrus wakens,
jade and silver begin to shiver.
A chorus of fluttering butterfly wings
enchant the forest
with whispered songs and salsa dances.

Friendship's Quiet Moments

Two rocking chairs face one another,
creaking in unison.
Pine boards aged by rain and snow
sing with locusts and crickets.

My friend and I wait
as lavenders drift off the edge of evening,
reflections of caring in each others eyes.

Blue windbreakers whisper around us
as smiles fill spaces between words not spoken.
Only sighs heard deep inside thoughts.

Slender, interlaced fingers
speak their own quiet language.
Compassion, interwoven with patience,
waits in the lap of silence.

Muscles relax into warm wax
speaking a thousand words.
Acceptance gracefully crosses her legs,
as a yellow rose opens in the garden.

My Universe Within

My ears assaulted:
musical limericks of cell phones,
screeching voices of the outraged,
blaring horns from the impatient,
boom boxes—gifts for hard of hearing.

Trucks roll past
with sounds of kettledrums.
Bass notes belch from oversized speakers
wrestling with each beat of my heart.
Yellow and blue cars streak into greens.

Hands clasped, I plead for calm.
My attention drawn to soft murmurs
from rustling oak leaves,
twitters from nature's sanctuaries;
in the distance hushed sighs of angels.

A door opens into my world
where laughter tickles
the bottoms of my feet,
smiles filling spaces between words,
and warm touches cool themselves
on the top of a mountain.

Sobering Choices

I feel the weight of steel
jog across my chest.
Sweaty hands leave smudges
on white paper stretched
across the exam table.

The room glistens in stainless steel,
Q-tips in jars, tweezers and rolled gauze.
Diagrams hang like Rodin sketches
on white canvas walls
to give eyes a place to focus.
Hope wrestles with fear painted in reds.

A rap on the door signals
judgment is about to enter,
a folder in his hand, with a single word
typed in bold print.

Framed in white, the verdict is read.
The word "cancer" dangles from his lips
heard in slow motion;
edges sharp and cutting.

Fear balances on the edge of a crevasse.
White lightning freezes the moment
into a still life photo
as flesh melts from bone.
Eyes burn, tears race
to extinguish the blaze.

Options, spread like butter
under a warm knife,
will retreat with me
into the loneliness of night.

If I Should Perish

An old maple stump,
center aged hollow,
supports my weariness.
Brown rings once circled its axis;
a language written for trees.

Long branches
clad in dark, leafy greens
once feasted on sunlight.
Deep musical notes echoed
from woodwinds,
piccolos played at the tops of trees.

I watched leaves change
from hunter green to yellow ocher
when whims of nature
changed seasonal wardrobes.

Rising from the stump,
my playground alive
with playful shadows of new maples
planted by the wind.
A smile peeks between wrinkles
on my face.

GREETINGS

A rising sun peeks through
a duvet of mist
into my bedroom window
reflecting a mirrored image
having unkempt hair,
a wrinkled nightgown,
and crow's feet printed
in corners of each eye.

Wishful in reflections,
I am guided in preparation for the day
with a drive thru body wash,
dangling earrings, lip liner
and darkened lashes.

Knee-torn dungarees
and opened-toed flip-flops
disguise the real me.
Oceans clothed in blues and greens
tip white hats on the surface
to acknowledge treasures held within.

MANUSCRIPT

A driving rain washed down sidewalks
into giant puddles.
I stomped up and down
in playfulness, splattering classmates
coming from school
dressed in loud angry voices.

Struggling through my teens,
swimming marathons across rivers
of cut glass, left deep scars.
Showing off in a floral pattern swimsuit,
two sizes too small,
my self-esteem wrestled to break free.

Looking back through a tear in the clouds,
I see where ragweed once rooted.
In their place, poppies and spring ephemerals;
a sweet smell still lingers.

My edges beginning to curl,
a pale sienna tint on brittle pages;
a manuscript of flesh, bound in love.

MAGICAL DWELLINGS

Rose and cream-colored sea shells
waxed smooth by ocean tides,
sit abandoned on sandy shores,
free housing for long-legged hermit crabs.

My cream colored flesh
is my residence.
I stretch onto a blue and red towel
allowing the sun to spray paint
my house a deep tan.

Dreams cast images around me,
skin smooth from pampering
by exotic kelps and ocean plants.
Strands of blond hair flow down my back
to lie upon a graceful tail.
A golden crown rests upon my head.

I slip into a turquoise sea.
My body and I swim among golden coral
and green scaled sea serpents.
Starfish wink from bony homes.
Tortoises let me rest on armor
of hexagon and polygon designs
painted green and dark umber.
Leathery smiles on toothless faces
cause a chuckle.

I feel edges of my daydreams dissolving,
startled to discover my home set ablaze.
Flesh no longer a pale cream
but sun painted to lobster red.
My sorry self slips back
into the cool, medicinal sea
in search of sympathy.

Share with Me Your Silence

Our eyes collide in a white mist
as I watch you prepare for our morning jog,
lacing up high-cut Nikes
over blue striped socks.

A pale green tee shirt hangs
wrinkled over narrow hips
to cover tan shorts, a bit too small;
a red baseball cap worn backwards.

I study your long and quickened strides,
watch you pause, for only a moment,
to dwell on an invasive thought.
Your private space tangled up
with unspoken desires.

Arms swing to beats in our feet
while muscles scream in silence.
I watch sweat seep into your collar
turning edges to dark green.

A sculptured grin contours your face
as we lean into a nearby elm.
Twinkles dot the middle of sapphire eyes
as you cool your thoughts
inside a morning breeze.

WHISPERS IN THE DARK

My eyes close
swallowing me in darkness,
alive with pulsing yellow and orange lights
breast stroking across galaxies under my lids.
Elusive sunspots darting
off the horizon's edge.

Hearing voices whisper nearby,
I use my hands to separate black curtains
to better see my guardians of thought
who debate right from wrong.
Judgment bites like red curry.
Vindication soothes
like chocolate swimming around my tongue.

My tender psyche, swathed in guilt,
struggles to hold to schooled values
as I bathe naked among earthly needs.
My "id" watches with delight
knowing Freud would love this.

My Shadow

A shadow puddles around my feet,
obedient in its quest to mimic
the object of its affections.

Always careful to avoid doors
that enter in, roofs that rise above,
or clouds that block the sun
causing evening to settle early.

This shadow is dark and foreboding,
unpredictable as it stretches
from now until sunset;
no smiles, tears or sweaty palms,
obedient to my every move.

When walking it lags behind
or bounces playful at my side.
When evening sneaks behind lavender hills,
it races to the finish, stretching long and thin.
Dipped in darkness,
it merges with shades of the unknown.

Shadow, shadow, where are you now?
My heart cries with unrest,
floating in dark undulating fluid,
captive to the mysterious obscurity of night.

BIRTHPLACE OF A PRAYER

I squint over a sparkling cobalt sea.
Waves somersault,
a child's game races to shore
in blue shorts and white hats.
Voices splash, tumbling onto white sand.

Shallow water magnifies
smooth shells clad in creams and tans,
homes to hermit crabs.
Life in the sea's inky depths hold their silence.

I float face up
in the ocean's womb.
Water courses between fingers and toes,
seeps into my ears, caressing my cheeks.
Hair, suspended in blond ringlets,
winks gold in the sun's reflections.

I am transported, weightless,
into a secret place
where eyes cannot follow;
a temple built without stone.
Prayers form on my lips,
seek the "who" in "I am."

Shimmer

A lake rests over oyster shell sand.
Waking up for an early swim
under an apricot sky,
I see yellow umbrellas hang motionless
near plastic chairs.

Wading to my knees
in a watercolor by Cézanne,
reflections of sienna rocks shimmer;
green-needled pines float
in front of cotton clouds streaked in gold;
playful as Puffins courting near shore.

A gust of wind shatters my masterpiece.
Light shimmers to the sand,
reeds bend and twist,
green lily pads rise and fall
over waves rolling onto shore.

Blue-green ripples huddle
in shadows around my knees
broken into fragments of stained glass.

Waiting at the Door

Fingers massage a weary forehead.
Inside, an eye, not round or hazel
opens when lashes close
gathering memories in the dark.

I focus on past footfalls.
Running barefoot on sandy beaches,
watching impressionists splash blues and greens
behind cresting white caps,
a Claude Monet saved to pictures.

Shades of gold from fall leaves
lie down under trees.
High-pitched laughter resonates
above the sting of sorrow.
Love tries to sneak by
grazing at the door of tomorrow.

I try to imagine
the postscript for today,
but am held captive by darkness.
In the distance a clock chimes
and today summersaults into yesterday.

ONLY NOW

I was not aware
the sun was blistering flesh
until it painted me in reds.
I cooled myself in a nearby brook
where blues and greens swirled around rocks.

I was not aware wind had fingers
until it plucked gold leaves,
stirring them among reds and browns;
a palette knife mixing paint
around my window well.

I thought I knew who I was
until I looked in a mirror
searching past silver hair and stretch marks
to find kaleidoscopic changes,
scarlet rubies of age tumbling
with yesterdays diamonds.

.

I thought I knew what love was
until my skin came alive,
tingling beneath a fluorescent moon
come into fullness,
arriving on the sweet breath
of evening's first meal.

Only now will I let you capture me
in a lush green forest
on a bed of white trilliums
where you speak to me in warm strokes;
a silence shadows share in passing.

Ashes at My Feet

I prod smoldering birch logs
with a long oak branch.
Life explodes into an orange glow,
pulsating amid shades of gray
inside my campfire.

Smoke stings my nose;
lapping flames dart skyward
holding darkness.
Tongues of fiery serpents taste the air.
Exploding sparks keep me at a distance
lest a hot ash find a place to rest.

Undaunted, I move closer,
drawn by leaping images among the flames.
Warm yellows and reds
dance on the blazing toes of ballerinas
across a shadow filled canvas.

The fire wanes,
gasps for a last breath of night air
until morning light removes its magic.
Remaining at my feet—a white ash,
playmate for the wind.

Risking the Unknown

Heavy fog blankets the lake.
Silver layers blend
between bleached grays of thistledown
swallowing a passing boat.

Unafraid, a loon calls
dressed in a white shirt and black yarmulke,
diving beneath the surface
to capture a yellow perch,
his morning meal.

Voices of osprey, blue heron and eagles
hold their silence
in an ashen sky;
wings tethered with uncertainty of flight.

The sun rises to kiss the mist,
water transformed from gray to turquoise.
Dew tears that cling to petals of water lilies
dissolve away.
My oars slice deep into the morning.

Painting with Words

With a sharp edged tool
I etch shapes of raccoons, owls and squirrels
into the surface of a stump.
Branches, leaves and robins
enjoy beauty in more than one dimension.

Walking past a farmer's pastured field,
buttercups greet me with open petals.
Placing delicate buds under my chin, I imagine
creamy butter melting on my neck.

I am drawn into their color,
rubbing pastels across a matte paper
with my little fingers,
blending ochre into tints and tones,
waking bees and hummingbirds
who circle the blush of yellow.

In my studio, I cut words from magazines
building a collage of black on white.
Words, thin, fat and bold
spread across tag board
where I arrange, rearrange and overlap.

Courage floats like scents of peonies
blooming in the backyard.
Phrases spring to life
as golds and indigos of sunset.

Wild Flowers in March

March ephemerals
awaken to sounds of a west wind.
Trilliums, saw-tooth violets and trout lilies
sleep beneath patches of snow
waiting for a last guttural roar from winter
before life stirs.

Violet, ochre and white buds dot the landscape.
Trilliums open white wings
sipping warmth
before forests build green canopies
to shade ferns and flowers.

Sateen and silk petals open,
spreading wide onto a bed
of last year's rust pine needles,
a birthing table for this year's offspring.
I bathe in smells from their invasion
like fresh cut grass.

Strolling through northern pines
and clump birch,
I watch stems turn from green to yellow,
heads bend low,
petals returning back to earth.

Bulbous wombs rest beneath compost
drawing nutrients for next year's delivery
when a flurry of colors
mixes with smells of pine—if only for a day.

When All the Veils Are Lifted

Who designs snowflakes,
doilies that dust my eyelashes
with geometric designs?
Who blueprints mackerel skies
with silver scales
racing to the horizon's edge?

Who gives voice
to long-tailed mocking birds
who sing among branches of cypress trees;
tall giants with roots that suckle
pond water from a freshened earth?

Who creates smiles
donned with a hundred meaning
or a thousand eyes stroking the landscape?
Few will see green-sequined hummingbirds
sipping from yellow tulips
or a spotted fawn camouflaged by tall grass.

Moving through a secret sky
I ride on whispers of wind.

Mysterious Light

Leaves painted viridian and oxide green
overlap at the top of poplars and pines,
leafing over the forest
in coverlets of darkness.

Eddies of lemon and gold
laser through tops of barren branches
onto the forest floor.
A pileated woodpecker raps for attention,
his red head awash in sunlight.

I am drawn towards this luminary,
where mosquitoes, nits and butterflies
flutter in a glistening pillar of light
reaching to the sun.

Breaching the edge between dark and light
I am drawn inside
to bathe in its buttery glow,
my hair changing into golden threads.

Sweet scents of lily milk and honey
rise from beneath my feet
inside this yellow flame
where tears no longer find a place to cry.

About the Poet

Joyce Uhlir received her BA in Art Education from Dominican College of Racine, Wisconsin at age thirty five. Teaching for several years in an elementary setting, she saw a need for children to express themselves through non-threatening media, like paint, clay and natural materials. Moving on, she worked two years at Norris Adolescent Center for adjudicated youth in Racine County near her home in Union Grove, WI. She later transferred to a treatment center in Milwaukee, working as an Art Therapist with exceptional education students. She earned her graduate degree in emotional disturbances from the University of Wisconsin.

Three years before retirement she transferred to a school for the gifted and talented with an emphasis on teaching to individual learning styles. As she became more proficient in her profession, she realized the importance of self expression balanced with the acquisition of knowledge.

It was only after retirement that she discovered poetry as a viable means to release thoughts and give meaning to expressions using words, a deficit she struggled with in her early years. With the help of her teacher, Diane Frank, who understood the importance of teaching through people's strengths, she grew into her role as poet at seventy five, using her gift of painting to transform her poetry into colorful expressions. She now facilitates and works with adults her age who, more than ever, need to release a lifetime of memories onto paper, using poetry as a means to expression.

www.ingramcontent.com/pod-product-compliance
Lightning Source LLC
Chambersburg PA
CBHW032034090426
42741CB00006B/810